# THERE YOU ARE

# BOOKS BY LOUIS SIMPSON

Poetry

*The Arrivistes: Poems 1940–49*
*Good News of Death and Other Poems*
*A Dream of Governors*
*At the End of the Open Road*
*Selected Poems*
*Adventures of the Letter I*
*Searching for the Ox*
*Caviare at the Funeral*
*The Best Hour of the Night*
*People Live Here: Selected Poems 1949–83*
*Collected Poems*
*In the Room We Share*
*Jamaica Poems*
*There You Are*

Literary Criticism

*James Hogg: A Critical Study*
*Three on the Tower: The Lives and Works of Ezra Pound,*
    *T. S. Eliot and William Carlos Williams*
*A Revolution in Taste: Studies of Dylan Thomas,*
    *Allen Ginsberg, Sylvia Plath and Robert Lowell*
*A Company of Poets*
*The Character of the Poet*
*Ships Going into the Blue*

Other

*Riverside Drive* (novel)
*An Introduction to Poetry*
*North of Jamaica* (autobiography)
*Selected Prose*
*The King My Father's Wreck* (memoirs)

# THERE
# YOU
# ARE

POEMS

Louis Simpson

STORY LINE PRESS ✦ *1995*

Published by Story Line Press, Three Oaks Farm,
Brownsville, OR 97327

This publication was made possible thanks in part to the generous
support of the Nicholas Roerich Museum, the Andrew W. Mellon
Foundation, the National Endowment for the Arts, and our individ-
ual contributors.

*Book design by Chiquita Babb*

Library of Congress Cataloging-in-Publication Data

Simpson, Louis Aston Marantz, 1923–
    There you are : poems / Louis Simpson.
      p.   cm.
    ISBN 1-885266-17-0 (alk. paper), — ISBN 1-885266-15-4
    I. Title.
  PS3537.I75T48  1995
  811'.54—dc20                           95-30259
                                           CIP

# ACKNOWLEDGMENTS

Poems were first published in these magazines. The author is especially grateful to Frederick Morgan and Paula Deitz, editors of *The Hudson Review,* who have published his writing over the years.

*American Poetry Review:* "The Liberated Characters' Ball."
*Cimarron:* "Society Notes."
*Colorado Review:* "Like a Glass of Tea."
*Harvard Magazine:* "A Genius in the Family," "The Door," "Remembering the Sixties," "Viet-Cong," "Shoo-Fly Pie," "Hawaii."
*Harvard Review:* "Two Friends," "Returning to Paris."
*The Hudson Review:* "Suddenly," "The Associate," "The Believer," "The Iverson Boy," "Stairs," "August," "Her Weekend in the Country," "Patsy," "Honeymoon."
*The New Criterion:* "To a Russian Poet," "The Choir Master's Evening Party," "The Cabin," "Working Out," "A Bayman," "The Indian Student," "The Poet's Pipe."
*New England Review:* "Fame."
*Princeton University Chronicle:* "Country."
*The Southern California Anthology:* "The Dental Assistant."
*The Southern Review:* "Al and Beth," "Outward Forms," "A Clearing."
*Sycamore Review:* "After a Light Snowfall."
*Tampa Review:* "There You Are."
*Visions:* "The Walker on Main Street," "The Yardman's Story."

"The Choir Master's Evening Party" was also published in *Jamaica Poems,* a limited edition, by The Press of Appletree Alley, Lewisburg, Pennsylvania.

"Old Field Stories" was published in *In Autumn: Contemporary Long Island Poetry* by Birnham Wood Graphics, Northport, New York.

*For Miriam, always*

# CONTENTS

*3*
*A Clearing*

THERE

YOU

ARE

## TO A RUSSIAN POET

"The yoke of Communism
has been lifted." Congratulations!
You're free to speak and write
your mind, and no one will call you
a parasite. You could be a celebrity.

And that will be what they like,
not your writing. Who has the time
to read these days? And the one thing
all parties, Left and Right,
agree on, is poetry . . . who needs it?

In today's unfettered economy
your poems will have to compete
with "the popular arts," i.e.
reruns of *I Love Lucy*.
Not much of a public for you . . .

When they have a hundred channels
they'll want to be entertained,
not made to think about "life"
and be sad and melancholy.
For, let's face it, that's what poems do.

You must forgo the meeting
where you recited and the next day
everyone in Leningrad would be talking . . .
"I know, 'Unruly Horses' . . .
but what did it really say?"

You'll be pouring your infinite riches
out in a little room,
to a homeless person who snores
and a woman who misread the schedule.
She thought this week was someone else.

It's your turn now to discover
the answer to the riddle:
what's the sound of one hand clapping?

# Objects of the Stream

We found among the objects of the stream certain feelings that hardly changed, that stood out warm and vivid in the past just as the present feeling does now.

*William James*

Mr. Cooper, the physics teacher,
was a cross-eyed little Englishman.
When he was angry he reddened
and shouted and spit flew.
He was also in charge of the choir
and would have us to his house.
We sang "The Londonderry Air,"
"What shall we do with the drunken sailor?"
and a song with the refrain,
"Oh no John, no John, no John, no!"
which was daring. Then Mrs. Cooper
who wore black ankle boots
came in and gave us tea and biscuits.

The evening came to an end
with a song about a dying swan,
and we walked back across the commons.
The moon stared through a window
on rows of beds. No talking
after "lights out." The diesel
labored in the night. The house master
coughed in his study. I lay
and listened to the roof beams creaking
in the wind from across the sea.

Nipkow and Cosulich
exported "seconds," merchandise
with small imperfections . . .
nylon stockings, ballpoint pens.
I packed them in cellophane,
then cartons, to be shipped
to Europe for their postwar legs
and literary movements.

Nipkow had a sideline, diamonds.
He would sit at his desk by the hour
holding a diamond up to the light
or staring at some little diamonds
in the palm of his left hand.
He'd rise and grind a diamond
on the wheel. Then put on his coat
and go to meet someone like himself
with whom he would exchange diamonds,
each of them making a profit
somehow out of this.

One day I suddenly quit.
Then I worked on the *Herald Tribune*.
A reporter would call "Copyboy!"
and one of us would run over
and take his copy to the horseshoe
where the Count, as we named him,
a bald head and rimless glasses,
presided over his crew.

One would read the piece in a hurry
and write a heading for it,
so many letters, to fit.

My greatest adventure
was going to the fourteenth floor
of the Waldorf Astoria
to fetch copy about the flower show
at Madison Square Garden.

I quit that job suddenly too.
"You didn't like the export business,"
said Sylvia Cosulich —
I was still seeing her
though her parents didn't approve —
"and you don't want to be a reporter.
What are you going to do?"

In the silence there were sounds
of the traffic down below,
the elevator opening.

                Suddenly
the room seemed far away.
I was looking through a window
at clouds and trees.

And looking down again
to write, as I am now.

They still haven't stopped talking
about Max and his ideas.
If every little itch you feel
throughout the course of a day
were to happen all at once . . .
"Think about it," he would say.

What is time? Where is it?
Inside our heads, where else.
So the greater the population
the more time there must be.
"New York is older than Jerusalem,"
he said. "It's commonsense."

# AL AND BETH

My Uncle Al worked in a drugstore
three blocks above Times Square,
dispensing pills and cosmetics.
All day long crazy people
and thieves came into the store,
but nothing seemed to faze him.

His sister, Beth, was the opposite . . .
romantic. She used to sing
on ships that sailed from New York
to Central and South America.
When the tourists came trailing back
on board with their maracas,
Beth would be in the Aztec Room
singing "Smoke Gets in Your Eyes"
and "I Get a Kick out of You."

Once when I argued with Al
about something that America
was doing . . . "My country
right or wrong," he told me.
I suppose so, if you've come
from a village in Russia no one
ever heard of, with no drains,
and on saints' days the Cossacks
descend on you with the blessing
of the Church, to beat out your brains.

And when, after a fortnight
being seasick, there's the statue,
and buildings reaching up
to the sky. Streets full of people.
The clang of a bell, someone yelling
as you almost get run over.
More things happening every second
in New York, than Lutsk in a year.

Al lived on Kingston Avenue, Brooklyn,
all of his life, with the wife
his mother had picked out for him.
Beth never married. She was still waiting
for Mr. Right.

Of such is the Kingdom
of Heaven. Say that I sent you.

# THE ASSOCIATE

## 1

I would read until I was sure
then type a report.
When it came back from J. J.
I'd write the letter of rejection.

"Don't go in for criticism,"
he said. "It gets you in trouble.
Use the standard form: 'We regret
that due to the limitations of our budget
et cetera et cetera.'"

One day he called me in.
From now on I wasn't just a reader,
I was to be an associate,
working with authors on their books.
The rise in status, unfortunately,
didn't carry a raise in pay,
due to the limitations
of our budget et cetera.

## 2

J. J. on the intercom . . .
she was with him now,
would I come right away.

The eyes she turned towards me
were like ice. "I want everything
put back just the way it was,"
she wrote to J. J.
"I haven't read my Joyce for nothing."

"Here's the culprit now," he said.
Turning to me . . . "Peter,
I know that you think as highly
of *Vows* as I do. It has greatness,
wouldn't you say? Sweep and vision?"

I had a vision of my paycheck
fading. I said yes.

              Then he and she
discussed the vanishing of greatness.
This morning's *New York Times*
carried G. B. Shaw's obituary.
"There's no one left," she sighed.

He placed a hand over hers.
"I don't agree. I may be just an optimist,
but when I read the opening pages
of *Vows*, I said to myself, J. J.,
this is it . . . what you've been hoping for."

Later, when she had left,
he spoke to me . . . as a friend.

Did I realize that all the while
I was with them I never once smiled?
It isn't enough to like to read,
you have to like people. Putting a hand
on my shoulder . . . "Stay loose."
A phrase from baseball . . . He liked the Yanks
but still rooted for Cincinnati.

"Smile," he said. I said that I would try.


## 3

I poured myself a double,
then made supper. The oven,
refrigerator, and sink
took up one whole wall.
The rest of the room was quite large.

Sometimes I ate out . . . with Gallagher.
Mike came to work at Albion House
the year after me. He too was divorced.
Now he was having an affair
with the wife of a fashion photographer.

He had a favorite eating place,
a diner on Third Avenue.
He said, "They make a very tasty steak."

The word "tasty" coming from Mike
with his build of an ex-football-player,
sticks in my mind. I can see his face,
his jaw muscles working . . .
and the diner. There's jazz on the jukebox
featuring Bix Beiderbecke.


*4*


New York wasn't the main office . . .
that was in Indiana.
We went there to present our books
to the salesmen, and pay our respects
to Mr. Sidney, the Old Man.

The town is a convention center.
Shriners, Knights of Pythias,
members of the American Legion,
fill the lobby and stand around
on the sidewalk.

                    There are three now.
One of them is leaning on a stick
that is electrically wired.
A goodlooking woman comes by . . .
he touches her with it and she jumps
out of her skin. Now she is trying

to hit him with her handbag.
"Take it easy, boys," says the policeman.

Their wives come with them.
I rode down in the elevator
with three. Their hair was blue-rinsed
the color of laundry detergent.
One was carrying a roll
of toilet paper. "Here, young feller,"
she said, and held it out to me,
"have a crap game." And all three
went into a fit of laughter.

We gave our book presentations.
Then there was lunch.
After lunch, more presentations,
with the salesmen, whose party this was,
falling asleep.

We came together again
for dinner. Between the courses
one of the salesmen, named Finneran,
walked around and stood behind you
and made a remark that was supposed
to be funny. He did this with everyone,
I noticed, except the Old Man.

Then there were toasts . . . to our  President,
Mr. Sidney. To the Vice-President
in Charge of Sales. To someone else
in charge of production.
Whereupon I rose to my feet.

There are things you have said and done
that haunt you for the rest of your life.
I hear myself making a speech,
saying that we should be grateful
to J. J., for being such a fine editor.

I see the eyes of the Old Man
glaring from the head of the table.
Alice, our publicity woman,
staring at me with wide eyes.
J. J. looking down at his plate . . .

I sit down again, knowing
what a fool I've made of myself.
"Who does he think he is?" says the voice
of Finneran, loud and clear.


5

I met Mike at Grand Central
and we took the train to Old Greenwich.

J. J. met us, the two boys with him.
The older boy seemed nervous.
He kept telling J. J.
to drive slowly and look out.

J. J. said there was a chore
he had to finish. Would we help.
I said that I would. Mike said
riding on the train had given him
a thirst.

' When we got to the house
Mike retired to the living room
with a drink. I helped J. J.,
holding the boards while he hammered,
making a kennel.

In the afternoon
some people came by. A woman
who ran an art gallery in Greenwich;
the lawyer who lived next door.
Betsy, J. J.'s wife, made hors d'oeuvres.
Mike and I took drink orders.

A woman who was "in theater"
talked about Judy Garland,
what a wonderful person she was
and how she was killed by drugs.
She ended saying, "We all failed her."

How did I fail Judy Garland,
I wondered, but did not say.
The remark hangs in the air
among other things that were said
that afternoon . . . not ideas
and sentences, but breaths of air
and sound waves, emanations.

✦

It's two hours later
and people are arguing about
politics . . . "That's how much you know!
Adlai Stevenson couldn't suck eggs."

"I've heard all I want,"
Betsy says, and makes for the door.
We hear her driving off
fast . . . a squeal of brakes.

Luckily it isn't a child
she's run over, just the dog.

6

There's a picture . . . like an electric chair.
You're to put your prospective mate

in the chair. A pointer moves
so many degrees.

You work out both your futures
from astrological signs.

Finally you ask, are the two of you
compatible?

I'm expecting an old lady
in tennis shoes. Instead
she's a rather attractive redhead,
if you like the girl next door,
with freckles, when she's thirty-five.

As I explain why "we regret,"
the elbow she has placed on the desk starts to rap,
and I notice that she's trembling
all over, from head to toe.

"I hear," she says, "you were in San Francisco.
What did they tell you about me?"

Finally she leaves. Bernice,
the office manager's assistant,
who shares the same cubicle, her desk facing mine,
and doesn't miss a word,
puts a forefinger to her temple
and rotates it . . . the immemorial sign
that means, "This person is crazy."

## 7

Walter the office manager
paces the floor continually.
The cubicle I sit in is enclosed
with frosted glass. I look up
and see, gliding above the line
of frost, a pair of eyes
watery and blue . . . in lenses
that make them look like oysters . . .
fixed on me with suspicion.
That's Walter. Am I working
or dreaming the time away?

One day, in a moment of exuberance,
I go into Walter's office
with a good review of one of our books
in the *Times*.

        "That's not good," he says.
"Now the author will expect us
to advertise."

        I return to my cubicle
and stand at the window
looking out. It isn't just writers
who are crazy.

We are on the twenty-third floor.
Two floors below there's a ledge

with heads . . . of gods and goddesses
where they can't possibly be seen.

It isn't just the world of publishing
that's crazy. It's the world.

## 8
### Bettina

It's 900 pages long.
"Cut 300," says J. J.

Then I am to try my hand
at three chapters in the style
of the author, to bridge the gaps.

I make an astonishing discovery.
Since the characters aren't mine
all sorts of ideas occur to me.
I reel off words with the facility
of Dumas or Walter Scott.

I have Bettina's husband lose her
in a dice game. What were the games
they played in the thirteenth century?
That's the kind of thing that would take me
days. . . . To hell with it! I'll make one up.

Then I have her leave the gambler
for a Scotsman, a soldier of fortune.
There'll be the siege of a castle . . .
crossbows, catapults, boiling oil.

Sex no longer presents an obstacle.
Every few pages
I take the clothes off Bettina.
No sooner does she get them on
than I start taking them off.

"Well done," says J. J. "I knew you had it in you."


9

He sits holding his manuscript
like a hurt child on his lap.
I hear my own voice far away.

Once, at the start of fall,
I was driving from New England.
The leaves were turning red and orange,
the air was fresh and cool.

I saw a sign for a barn sale.
It was dark inside. After a while
as my eyes grew accustomed
I saw tables heaped with tools,

another with cups and saucers.
There were toys and souvenirs . . .
the glass ball that you shake
to make snowflakes swirl and fall.

A staircase led to a second floor
with furniture and, to one side,
bookcases, shelves of books . . .
joke books by Bennett Cerf
cheek by jowl with the Civil War.
A row of best-sellers
in the *Reader's Digest* shortened versions . . .
books that had once been praised
and now were, most of them, forgotten.
Who now reads Bulwer Lytton?
Van Wyck Brooks? Josephine Herbst?

And here's another writer.
What shall I say to him?
That life is far more wonderful
than anything we can write?

That's not what he wants to hear.
"But listen to me. Let me tell you,"
he would say, "about my life."

The concierge climbed five flights
to  complain. Erich was on the stairs,
just coming up. "Throw her down,
Vicki," he shouted,  "I'll catch her!"

There were good times in Paris.
That was before the war,
of course, and La Rafle.

A girl came into the room.
She went over to Erich
and put an arm around him.
"I've done all my homework,
Papa. Can I go now?"

"Lisa is an American girl,"
he said. "Already she has boyfriends."

✦

La Rafle. I looked it up.
A policeman comes to the door . . .
"Monsieur, you and Madame
and the children must be packed
and report yourselves to the stadium
tomorrow by seven o'clock."

So tomorrow, there you are.
And they walk you to the station

and give you to the Germans
with a list of names, and two fingers
to the cap. Signing off.

From there by train to Drancy.
Then Auschwitz, the last stop,
"letzter Termin," and the gas.

✦

It's late, and I'm hurrying
to pack. I have to catch up.
The streets are full of bicycles
going to work. Then I'm running.

And then, with a sense of relief,
I see them up ahead.
There must be thousands moving
like a river through the street.

Some with big suitcases,
looking well dressed and well fed,
others as though they've been living
under a bridge for weeks.

I shout, "Where are you going?"
"To the station!" they shout back.

# TWO FRIENDS

His wife came from New Hampshire.
She was beautiful and rode horses.
I went with them once to a horse show
in Greenwich. Jo rode a Tennessee Walker.
It was sheer delight to see her
put the big beast through his paces:
how he'd lift a hoof slowly
like a guardsman, and set it down.

But then they were divorced,
and Mike lived by himself
in a railroad flat in the Village
that smelled of whiskey and garbage,
with dishes in the sink and on the floor.
He sat with his fly open, talking
about women, you couldn't live with them.
In the middle of the diatribe
he would fall asleep and snore.

Then he was having an affair
with the wife of a fashion photographer.
I've written about it elsewhere:
how she would take off her clothes
at a party or in a bar,
and how she and Mike quarreled
and he sliced her with the breadknife . . .
twenty-six stitches.
Our editor in chief, J. J.,
put up bail, and Sandra refused

to press charges, so Mike got out of it.
Years later she wrote a novel . . .
the critics liked it but it didn't sell.

✦

Then he married a German woman
named Lottie. It was said
that she came of the nobility
and escaped just ahead of the Russians.
Mike asked me to be the best man,
and afterwards I gave a toast.

A man who worked at Random House
drew me aside. "Don't you know?"
Mike was just doing her a favor.
Now she wouldn't have to go back,
being married to an American citizen.
He looked at me with a smile
and I remembered why Mike and I
disliked him. So that was why
people had laughed when I said,
"To Mike and Lottie, may
they live happily ever after."

✦

I knocked and went in.
J. J. said, "I'm glad you came.

Mike told me about it.
I told him I'd have preferred
to hear it from you."
He put a hand on my shoulder:
"It's not the end of the world,
but next time something comes
from Hilary, I want to see it.
He's the best literary agent in town."

That should have been the end
of my acquaintance with Mike,
but I think I'm emotionally lazy,
if there is such a term. In any case,
this was on a Friday. That evening
we met at the White Horse as usual.

There was a poet holding court
to a circle of admirers.
Afterwards as we walked
to the Blue Mill, Mike recited
"Jabberwocky," in what I thought
a hilarious imitation
of a resonant Welsh voice.

✦

He came to work later
every day. Then he'd go out,
and when he came back he'd been drinking.

He'd slump in his chair and snore.
So finally they let him go.

And then there was an opening
for an editor-in-chief
at King Publishers, and J. J. went.
The Vice-President in Charge of Sales
hinted broadly I might leave too,
so I did, and went into teaching,
and moved to California,
and years went by, as they do.

◆

"Dear Peter,

I've been talking to the doctor,
and I feel a need to settle
old accounts, things on my mind.
Do you recall the book you rejected
that went on to win the N. B. A.?
I told on you to J. J.
And once when you came to my place
I took some money out of your jacket.
You'll find ten dollars enclosed.

And there was a waiter in Syracuse
I stiffed. But why involve you
in my crimes. I've thought about it,

how you would stand in for me
at Albion House when I was missing
or hungover.

My wife Betty
and I have bought a house
in Roscommon, more like a castle.
She came into money from her family,
and we feel the same way about Ireland,
so we came and bought the house.
We're fixing it up . . . who knows
when the work will be finished.
People here have a different idea
of time, they like to stretch it out.

I've been reading 'Ecclesiastes'
on the wise man and the fool.
It says they'll both be equal
in the end — they'll both be forgotten.
And, which you wouldn't expect
from the Bible, it tells you
to eat, drink, and be merry.
So don't try to be too wise,
and give my regards to the White Horse.

As ever

Mike

your friend"

## VIET-CONG

One moonlit night in Quinhon
they were standing at the window
when she grasped his arm. "Viet-Cong!"

By moonlight he sees them still,
in black pajamas flitting
like cats from roof to roof.

If I close my eyes I can hear
the voice of Mario Savio . . .
Aptheker, a voice like a corncrake,
and Weinberg: "Don't trust anyone
over thirty."

        Where's he now?
According to the *New York Times,*
on Wall Street, making money—
"innocently employed" as someone,
I think Doctor Johnson, said.

We marched for peace from Berkeley
to Oakland, carrying candles.
It was dark on the way back.
The candles went singly glimmering
down side streets, and went out.

# RETURNING TO PARIS

*Paris change! mais rien dans ma mélancolie*
*N'a bougé!*

Paris changes, said Baudelaire.
He also said that his melancholy
never changed. I suppose so . . .
but still, he lived in Paris.

I used to have a bad dream.
I'd be walking in Paris.
It was growing dark, and time
to leave, or I'd miss my train
and the boat. I was leaving Paris
and would never be back again.
Now, if you like, that's melancholy!

But in fact I've been back
many times. And recently
Miriam and I found ourselves,
I could swear, on the very street
of my dream . . . doors and windows
shut tight, and not a living thing
in sight but a man who was sitting
on a bench all by himself.

Then there was a street with shops
and crowds of people looking
for bargains . . . in shoes
and dresses, sets of dishes.

Then the rents became higher
and the things in the windows

expensive: evening clothes,
Japanese cameras, Italian handbags.
There was a big department store,
a bank, and we were there,
in the middle of Paris, with cars,
motorcycles and buses
rushing around.

We sat down
and looked at the signs for watches
and chocolate and perfume.
And the people . . . the important man
wearing glasses with black frames.
The English or German couple
in shorts, with a pack on their back,
and big hiking boots. The elegant woman.

✦

And here we are again,
on a bridge, looking upstream
at the fly-boats coming down.

Loitering by a bookstall,
dipping into ancient history
and philosophy . . . ideas
that once were the rage in Paris:
Sartre, Heidigger, de Man,
soiled, for just a few francs.

And one of my favorite poets,
with his bandaged head and smile.
Shelled silly. He reminds me
of Sam.

        When the French students
were throwing pellets of bread
at each other, "It's a sacrilege
to waste good bread!" he shouted.

I could have crawled under the table.
I can see the faces in the restaurant
turned toward us. The face
of the woman sitting across from me,
her eyes wide open, her fork
suspended in mid-air.

Silence. Then a horn blows,
and I'm standing on a sidewalk
with Miriam, waiting to cross.

# The Walker on Main Street

**2**

Speketh so pleyn at this time, we yow preye,
That we may understonde what ye seye.

THE CANTERBURY TALES

A woodpile and a fence,
grass, a hedge, a screen of trees . . .
I wish I had romantic neighbors
to talk about, like the lady
Yeats speaks of. When she was offended
by a farmer, her serving man
ran out with the garden shears
and brought her the farmer's ears
in a little covered dish.

I have no man to serve me,
but once, offended by the lout
who lives across the street,
I quarreled with him, loudly.
When his wife put her head out
and said, "Peter, I don't like your language,"
I replied, on the moment's thought,
"And I don't like your face."
We haven't been troubled by them since.

Yeats created Hanrahan,
the mighty lecher. What
lust-driven, legendary man
shall I summon? Where we live
there are no legends, only gossip.
Yet the great matter of Troy
that ended with a whole town burning
began with an inch of skin
between a woman's skirt and stocking.

I give you my friend Roger
who recently left Denise
and is living with Diane
in a motel in Florida.
Watching daytime television . . .
Mosquitoes and tractor trailers
keeping him awake, making his heart race,
like a clashing of shields
and swords, and flights of arrows.

# THE DOOR

They still talk about the Wagners
who used to live in our house.
Henry Wagner planted trees,
mainly evergreens: spruce, sequoia,
holly, monkey puzzle, magnolia.

His wife would drive to the village
and bring someone back to drink with her.
There were drunks sleeping over,
and fights, with someone running
to take refuge at a neighbor's house.

Then Fred Ward came and stayed.
Henry said, "You two are more suited
to each other," and he left.
The door up on the second floor
with pieces gouged and hacked out of it,

that was Caroline Wagner, trying
to get at Fred with a chain saw.
There are a lot more stories.
We should talk to Emily Ainbinder,
they say. Emily knows them all.

This year there's a belly dancer.
The boys take turns going up to her
where she stands, rolling her belly
and ringing her fingerbells.
The idea is to stick a bill
in her waist, between the elastic
and the moisture and heat of her skin.

A face across the room reminds me
of someone I used to know,
so I go over and greet him warmly.
He doesn't know what to make of it.
He's with the Better Bay Foundation. . . .
"Why are you asking me these questions?
Why are you calling me Sam?"

She comes once a week . . . and talks.
Her husband, Jim, is an invalid.
Up to six years ago
a healthy, goodlooking man,
now it exhausts him just to walk
from his chair to the dinner table.

He is irritable and shouts at her
then says that he's sorry.
The worst thing is, he expects her
to drop whatever she's doing
and bring something. He's watching TV
with the boys, and calls to her, "Eadie,
would you bring a glass of water."
He wouldn't think of asking the boys.

She takes her paraphernalia
to the bathroom: bucket and mop,
Tilex for the walls, Bon-Ami
for the bathtub and sink. Ammonia
for the toilet. Thirty minutes later
reemerges and resumes.

"You ought to treat him," said her mother-in-law,
"with more consideration."
"What do you want me to do?"
she said. "Sit beside him and hold his hand,
and cry all day long?"

She belongs to the Church of the Redeemer
and believes she will be saved,
and that all the people she cares about
will be saved too. It stands to reason
if you're a believer, don't it?
And I have to agree, it does.

# THE IVERSON BOY

I met the Iverson boy
on the road. Boy? He has to be thirty
if a day. He crossed over,
faced me, and grabbed hold
of my hand. While I was trying
to get it back . . . "I am glad to see you,"
he said. "How long has it been?"

I said, "I don't know." He released my hand.
"I'm staying till four o'clock on Sunday,"
he said, "visiting my parents."
"They must be glad to see you."
"I suppose so." He looked me earnestly
in the face . . . "They haven't been saved."

✦

I had a friend whose wife
worked in the psychiatric division
at St. Anne's.

                The doctors were having a tournament,
table tennis. Just as the winning point
was hanging in the balance,
Tommy Iverson came barging
through the door. They could have killed him.

"What got to me," said my friend,
"was that when my wife told the story

she was full of sympathy for the doctors
and laughed at the poor *schlemiel*.
I thought, Why am I married to this person?"

✦

When I returned from my walk,
"Guess who I ran into,"
I said to Miriam, "the Iverson boy."
"Yes? What did you talk about?"
"His parents. They haven't been saved."

When we first came to live in the area
the Iversons had us to dinner.
John said that Richard Nixon
was one of the finest presidents
America ever had.

              And after a morning
with Sylvia, Miriam told me
she hadn't a brain in her head.
All that she seemed to care about
was television game shows.

Maybe that was what her son
thought she needed saving from,
shows like *Jeopardy* and *Wheel of Fortune*.

# THE DENTAL ASSISTANT

She has a steady boyfriend . . .
he wants to get married,
she doesn't think they ought to yet.
(She tells me this while adjusting
the headrest, clipping a napkin
at the back of my neck.)

                         Another thing,
he's a couch potato . . . sits for hours
switching from channel to channel.

Then Dr. Weiss comes in
and asks how are we today,
and that's the end of friendly conversation.
From here on, the sound of the tube
sucking, the whine of the drill . . .

I wonder if she and her boyfriend
will work out their differences.

Sex. It usually is.

He would be wearing an overcoat
no matter what the season,
a hat, a scarf, and gloves.
The same on a hot day in July
as on the coldest winter day.

He appeared at the top of Main Street
and walked down it, swinging his arms,
speaking to no one. At the harbor,
right turn on Broadway. Right again
on East Main, past the antiques
and The Good Times. Right again
by the post office, and so back
out on Main Street, to 25A.

He came every day one summer,
to the astonishment of strangers.
If any of them asked . . . "Oh yes,"
we'd say, and go back to whatever
we were doing before they asked.
They were strangers, he was one of us.

He used to appear around noon.
One day the clocks showed twelve,
twelve-thirty, and still no sign.
At one o'clock, J. K. Ashby Junior
came out and stood on the sidewalk.
He was joined by Pete from Moore's Market
and Judy from Her Ideas.

They looked the street up and down,
they looked at one another,
shook their heads, and went back in.

He has never been seen since.
But sometimes, after a good dinner
when people start to reminisce,
the man in the overcoat comes walking
quickly, speaking to no one,
always in the same direction
for a reason only known to him.

He talked about his son.
Tom had never been sick in his life. . . .
One day, up at the college,
he climbed five flights of stairs
and suddenly collapsed and died.
It seems that one side of the heart
was much larger than the other.

Stairs, he said as he measured . . .
When you build them you have to be sure
they're exactly the same height,
for when you step up or down
"the eye makes an adjustment."
If one is slightly higher or lower
you'll stumble.

He stands in the muddy area
where the stairs will be, writing numbers
with a pencil on the wall.
We'll have a devil of a time later
getting them off with soap and water.
But we forgive him. He is a man
with a great deal on his mind.

# THE YARDMAN'S STORY

"O mercy!" to myself I cried,
"If Lucy should be dead!"
                                   *Wordsworth*

Matt the yardman is here
with his big yellow John Deere
with five-speed transmission
and reverse. It's over-engined:
when you get it up in third or fourth
you're either walking too fast
or you're jogging. And all the parts
are made of steel. It can weigh
like a ton when you're mowing all day.

He likes landscape gardening.
Verna calls it cutting grass,
but it beats working in the store
in New York City.
                        "One night
we're getting ready to close
when a guy comes into the store.
Frank comes over. 'Keep an eye
on this one,' he tells me,
as if he had to. If it's wine
they're looking for, they go over
to the shelves and stay there
looking for a thirty dollar label
for five dollars. If it's whiskey
they make straight for their brand,
pay, and leave. But when somebody
comes in and just walks around . . .

Verna goes to powder her nose,
so that leaves Frank and I.
Here it comes now. The guy
goes over to the register
with a bottle. Frank
tells him how much. The guy
reaches in his coat and comes up
with a revolver. That's when
Verna comes back, sees the guy
waving the gun, and runs out again.
He yells 'Stop!' and runs after her,
but she's out the back door, running.
Me and Frank go out the front.
There's a police car cruising . . .
we hail it and they pick up the guy.

When I saw Verna turn round
and start running, I thought,
what if anything should happen
and I never saw her again?

She felt the same way about me,
she said. So we were married,
and moved here, to the country,
and the hell out of New York."

A middleaged man named Doherty
had the locker next to mine.
A detective. He showed me
scar tissue near his heart
where a bullet had gone in.

A new member joined, a woman
who was doing physiotherapy.
She was beautiful to watch
at Leg Curl and Leg Extension,
straddling a bench or lying down.

The tone of the whole place changed.
When she came, Doherty would run over
and be solicitous:
how was she feeling today,
and she mustn't overdo it.

Then she no longer came, she was cured,
and everything reverted:
the young men blowdrying their hair
assiduously, the old
telling their dirty stories.

And Doherty working out
at Pullover, Double Chest,
and Torso Arm . . . lifting weights
as though it were he or they
in a struggle to the death.

He walks backward across the deck
pulling the rake, working it up and down,
then brings up the rake head
and empties it on the cull rack.

This gray rubber ball
is a sea cucumber. And this,
a scungili — they eat the seed clams,
next year's catch, shell and all.
A square blue bottle, medicinal,
some Yakov's magic elixir.
He has a collection of old bottles,
and clay pipes, just the bowls,
dropped in the bay by Englishmen
two hundred years ago.

There are three littleneck clams
and a cherrystone. He puts the "necks"
in a red net bag. The cherrystone
on the deck, to one side.

✦

A bag of littlenecks, one hundred pounds,
fetches sixty-five dollars in today's market.
Not exactly the wealth of the Indies.
And the rake handle sections get pitted
and have to be replaced,
and the rake head twice a year.

Five years ago, many of the guys
left the bay — they couldn't make a living.
But he stuck it out. He's been a bayman
twenty-seven years, taking time out
for the army and a tour in Vietnam.
He couldn't wait to get back to the bay.

His wife understands — he couldn't do it
without her. Rita has a part-time job.
They own the house, and never buy anything
on time . . . never had a new car.
You have to stay away from monthly payments.
There are months, in winter, you don't catch anything.

✦

It can get pretty hairy
when the temperature goes down
and there's a wind from the northwest.

The gulls circle squawking.
One will light and stand there all day,
but not if there's a second person.
It's not that they're anti-social,
but they don't like dealing with the public.

One winter he lent a hand
in his brother's catering business
when one of the drivers took sick.
The longest two weeks of his life.

Over there is Blue Point, where the oysters
used to be. The salinity killed them.
Clams too are harder to find.

But to spend all your time figuring
how to make more money . . .

What for?

I said, "I can't talk to you
this morning, I'm very busy."
He jumped back two paces,
and smiled and said, "You have
a very pleasant irascibility."

I said, "Come to my house
on Saturday. You can tell me
everything on your mind, all at once."

So there we were, in my study,
with his father, the Sanskrit scholar
who died at twenty-three,
the uncle who kept a "dramshop,"
another uncle who was poisoned,
and a cousin named Maya. . . .

"Stop!" I said. "Go back
to the uncle who was poisoned."
"Yes," he said, "by his mistress."

He spoke in a monotone
of the village where he grew up
and, when he was a man, in Calcutta,
sharing a room above the market . . .
a shuffling all night long
going by, a murmur of voices.

✦

A book came in the mail, from India:
cardboard covers and cheap paper,
*Wings of Song* by Sastri,
dedicated to his "friend and mentor."

In India when someone chooses you
as his mentor, from then on
you're in his debt, obliged
to help him . . . find him a job.
When he marries you're expected
to help support his family.

There's no end to it . . . the quarreling
next door. The sound of a flute,
and a murmur and shuffling.

All those people in the street
who stay up all night long.

He is querulous and constipated,
Whitman tells us, but he still writes
a song every day of his life.

There is plenty to write about
in Old Field where we live.
Last night the constable phoned
the animal warden. "There's a rabbit,"
he said, "that's acting strange."

It was moving very slow.
Then she saw a pair of eyes
up the road, The fox.
It must have chased the rabbit
and tired it out.

As I said, lots of stories,
and some strange ones. But few occasions
for song, as far as I know.

People drive on summer nights
and park by Walter's place.
They neigh like a horse, and bark,
and neigh. Local boys
with a girl they want to impress.

Walter was going on a journey
for a month. He gave his man
instructions: "Every night
tether the horse and goat
and chain the dog."

            He returned
to find the hired man gone . . .
the horse, the goat, and the dog
on the ground, stretched stiff and cold,
each at the end of a chain.

That is why you hear those sounds.
At the end of summer they stop.

✦

Here come the fire engines;
the high school band from Shoreham;
a float with blue serge suits
and women in white. "Jesus Christ
Is Our Savior," the banner says.

At the tail of the parade
there's always a boy on a bicycle
making circles, showing off.
It isn't a boy, it's Gloria Wilmott,
Avery Wilmott's wife!

On a kid's tricycle,
pedaling, playing the clown,
backside low to the ground,
her knees up in the air.
People are stopping to stare.

You don't see such nice knees
every day, and such despair.

✦

Harry and I and Ted
were reading our poems.
First, Harry read his.
Ted didn't like the images,
they were "essentially dead."

His own was about a poet
who died in a Spanish jail.
"How can you care about him
when you're trying to kill yourself,"
Harry said, "with all that whiskey?"

Mine would be next. This impressed
the time and place on my mind:
the simple farmhouse furniture,
the sounds of a summer night
outside . . . frogs and cicadas.

Branches of a tree that flickers
with light. A sense of rain.

Gulls float on the Sound,
geese and ducks swim close to shore,
the reeds are growing tall in August.

As you round Cannon Bluff
the harbor spreads before you:
the ferry to Connecticut
either coming in or going out;
restaurants, fast-food places
and boutiques for the summer crowd.
The hospital, St. Anne's, large and yellow
on a hill to the west, looking down.
On the other side, to the east,
the Islandwide Lighting Company:
three chimneys like three sisters,
two of them tall and slender,
the third one short and stout.

There is everything you could want
on Main Street: a Chemical Bank,
drugstore, furniture store, newsagent.
A woman arranging dresses
in the window of Dillman's.
A man unloading cases of beer
from a truck. A woman passes . . .
he watches her as she walks away.

So it goes, day by day,
except when there's a traffic accident.

Or when a woman from Smithtown
and another from Miller Place
are arrested for petty larceny; when unknown
assailants throw a rock
through the rear sliding glass door
of a home on East Meadow Road;
when vandals tear up sods and dump garbage
on the twelfth green of the Oakwood Golf Course.

Then there will be an editorial
in *Suffolk News* on the rise of crime,
and Reverend Hunt will deliver his sermon,
"Watchman, what of the night?"
(There were incidents of vandalism
in Palestine long ago.)

But most of the time most people
lead decent, productive lives.
And there's plenty to see and do
on the calendar of events:
the North Shore Pro Musica
at the First Presbyterian Church;
a Pottery Demonstration;
a Two Day Conference on Exporting.

✦

There was a wind coming in gusts
from the sea, humid and warm,

and the hand ceased from typing,
the mower from mowing his lawn.

It was raining when night came,
and the wind still rising. Branches
tossed, and the leaves were rushing,
tormented, this way and that.
There was a sound high in the air
like the passing of an express train.
A tree fell with a tearing sound
and crack, and the lights went out.

We sat in the dark with a candle
and listened to the wind,
and thought of those who were lying
in endless night, forgotten
as though they had never been.
And the wind said, Be afraid
and know yourselves.

           So saying,
the great wind turned outward,
and with a distant rumbling
as of boxcars being moved,
returned to the sea where it came.

# DAVE, ERNIE, EDOUARDO

Dave climbs the tree.
He loops his rope round a limb,
throws the loose end over
another limb . . . it falls
to Ernie and Edouardo.

He saws off the limb.
It swings away, and they
haul on the rope like sailors,
jockeying the limb clear
of the house, bringing it down.

Dave and Ernie are talking.
Dave has a girl friend, Diane.
One of the men where she works
told her she has beautiful eyes.
"They're your selling point," he said.

"They know how to make you jealous,"
Ernie says, the voice of experience.
Edouardo as usual doesn't say anything.
He came here from *Mejico.*
He just drags brush and looks wise.

# HER WEEKEND IN THE COUNTRY

My wife's sister is visiting
for the weekend. Never again!

She can hardly wait to be back
in her apartment in Sutton Place . . .

East 56th Street,
a walk to the United Nations.

She's bored with the chatter
about people she doesn't know . . .

old copies of *The New Yorker,*
the glassed-in porch with a view

of snowflakes lightly falling
on grass and a child's swing.

When the Whip is still and the Ferris wheel
hangs in the air unmoving,

and PRINCESS MY-IMMBA & Her Very Talented
& Versatile Baboons are asleep,

and so is Johnny the hell driver
THE THRILL OF A LIFETIME

HELL DRIVING with a Dodge Pick-Up Truck
hurtling 70 feet through space . . .

then her voice calls from a mountain
on the wind like a widow ghost,

crazy for feeling so lonely
and crazy for loving you.

Uncle Bob prayed over the groom:
"Let him establish Kingdom principles."
Aunt Shirley prayed for the bride:
"Father, I pray an anointing on her."
"Love," said Reverend Philips,

"is insensitive, love is invalueless."
He said that we merger together
in holy matrimony,
and the choir burst into song:
"He waits for us, and waits for us."

✦

Every day they went swimming in the pool
and rode the two water scooters.
They rented two deck chairs
and sat on the sand in the sun.
A breeze made the palm leaves whisper.

The sea is green close to shore,
further out it is blue.
The ship standing still on the horizon
makes you think of sailing away
forever with the one you love.

✦

Jennifer ordered the roast beef platter.
Mike had the fish cakes.

"I thought you didn't like fish,"
she said. "Well," he said, "I guess you were wrong."
Tears came to her eyes. The honeymoon was over.

But then they went to their room
and everything was OK.
In the evening they went dancing
and stayed up late on the veranda
looking at the lights and the moon.

✦

And you, *hypocrite lecteur,*
what makes you so superior?

# A Clearing

The Third State is a grace that can only be achieved by renouncing all desires, by standing under the night sky sans age, sans sex, sans time, sans race, sans everything.

But who is capable of standing thus?

*Amos Oz*

The street used to be full of carriages,
but today the "house of fiction"
lies abandoned. Hardly anyone goes there.

I see the characters as lost,
wandering in corridors, or on the moors.
"I'm over here, by a wall!"
"Bloch here! I seem to have fallen into a ditch."
"Miss Bate here! Where *is* everyone?"

Or else, as the page never turns,
they have to stay where they are,
in a storm, or passionate embrace,
or in the middle of a war.
Imagine being in the retreat from Caporetto
forever! Or in a novel by Marryat,
pitching and rolling, eternally seasick.

Or with one of Hardy's comic characters
who speaks a Dorsetshire dialect.
Or in a room by Robbe-Grillet
with no one to talk to, only the furniture.

✦

Here's a happier thought:
they could be having a ball
with the disappearance of the "reading public."

I can see it . . . curtains drawn,
chairs pushed against the wall,
flutes and fiddles tuning up.
There's Natasha,
of course . . . Becky Sharp
and Emma. She hasn't had much fun
since she was out with Kugelmass.

Now they are free to be themselves.
That plain, seafaring man, for instance,
Conrad would never let him talk,
just tap on his barometer.
But now he's talking, a mile a minute . . .
not just talking, he's doing imitations:
"Tell me, plizz, my dear James,
how you say 'je ne sais quoi' in English?"

✦

Some have come from a fox hunt,
others from starving in a garret.
There are Russians, talking about their souls.
There's Manon, one of my favorites.

And, you'd scarcely recognize her . . .
from the middle of the nineteenth century
to the middle of this, poor Miss Havisham
sat with her wedding cake, clamped to a chair!
It gave her terrible indigestion.

But now she's changed . . .
no more mooning over "feelings"!
She's become entirely postmodern.
She lives with a friend who's a neurologist
and is taking a degree herself, in internal medicine.

There are a thousand like her.
And think of all who have been set free
from courses in creative writing.
Now they don't have to "stay in character"
or "contribute to the plot."

Laughing and shouting, kicking up their heels
at the liberated characters' ball!

One day during his office hour
a young woman appeared. "I'm Merridy,"
she said, "Merridy Johnson.
I'd like you to read my poems."

He said that he didn't teach writing.
"But couldn't you just look
and tell me, are they any good?"

She was carrying a flat white box.
She removed some tissue paper,
lifted out an album with a red cover,
and handed it to him carefully.

The poems were written in green ink
with flowers and birds in the margins.

She said, "What do you think?"
He said there were some nice images.
"Where?" she said, and leaned to see.

✦

His wife didn't go to poetry readings.
He went by himself, and sat at the rear.

But this evening he stayed to the end
and went to the reception afterwards
at Professor "Pat" Melrose's house.

When he arrived the poet was reciting
again, to a circle on the floor.
Merridy patted a place beside her
and he sat.
    Her eyes were shining.
Poetry gave her goosebumps.
Taking his hand she showed him where.

Melrose was a poet himself.
And there was nothing professorial
about these evenings. They were . . . bohemian.

Melrose's wife, a little woman
with a face like a rhesus monkey's
went around the room winking and grimacing.
"The pot's in the kitchen, acid's in the study"
she said with an eldritch laugh.

   ✦

He was stoned, and so was she,
going down Spruce Street
with a moon in the redwoods
and San Francisco glittering
on the bay, through the fog.

The poetry was great, she thought.
"As great as Bob Dylan's?"

But irony was wasted on her,
she was innocent. Like her room
with its posters of Joan Baez
and, right on, Bob Dylan.

Her books . . . *Siddhartha*, Ferlinghetti,
Alan Watts and Suzuki on Zen.
They spoke for her generation
like the *Poems, Sacred and Moral*
of a mid-Victorian girl.

And as softly as saying her prayers
she murmured, "Let's go to bed."

✦

Sam Mendelson was a font of wisdom.
He knew there was going to be an opening
for a medievalist at Ohio,
and who was sleeping with whom.
He said, "But they don't do it here.
They go to San Francisco."

The MLA was meeting in San Francisco.
There were sessions he had to go to,
Henry told his wife, Cynthia,
all very boring but unavoidable.
He'd be back in three days.

He and Merridy walked all over.
They ate at Fisherman's Wharf
and rode on a trolley.
They explored Chinatown,
and went dancing at Whisky a Go-Go.
He took her to The Hungry I
and they saw *Doctor Zhivago*.

✦

"Cynthia," he said, "I'm home!"
No answer. He went upstairs,
unpacked his suitcase, came down,
and was settling in with a scotch
in front of *The Untouchables*
when he had what he could only describe
as a sinking feeling.

He took the stairs two at a time.
No, her dresses were in the closet,
her doodads still on the table.

She came through the door
minutes later. She'd been shopping.
"How was the MLA?"

He gave her a circumstantial account
of the sessions he'd attended
in Yeats and Pound and Eliot.

"I had a vision," she said.
"I saw you in a room with a woman
as clearly as you're sitting here."

And he had always thought of her
as a person of limited imagination!

✦

He was up for promotion, to associate
with tenure.

          "Melrose is out to get you,"
Sam said. "Can you think of a reason?"

Henry thought. He shook his head.

"Did you insult Mrs. Melrose?"

"I don't recall. I may have."

At the meeting to decide his fate —
they're supposed to be confidential
but someone always tells —
Melrose spoke.

          His only concern
was in the area of collegiality.
"Associate" . . . think what that means.

Someone you have to your house,
introduce to your wife . . .

If the fathers and mothers of the children
to whom we stand *in loco parentis*
were here, they would ask, they would demand to
        know,
not is he supposed to be clever
and did the *New York Times* or some other publication
give a book a good review,
but is he a moral man?

Henry wasn't promoted and he didn't get tenure.

✦

That was why he was at the MLA.
He was being interviewed at five
by a man from upstate New York.
They had a place for a lost soul
somewhere in the Finger Lakes,
teaching rhetoric.

                "I've never taught it,
but I don't suppose it matters.
I've been speaking it all my life."
He laughed nervously. "Shall we have another?"

But I had to go. We were interviewing
on the fourteenth floor.

        "You're just in time,"
said the Chair. "Mrs. Harris
is going to tell us about her dissertation
on women's writing."

        "Ms Harris,"
she said. "The title is *Theory
and Praxis in Feminist Criticism*."
In a little while it became obvious
we weren't interviewing her, she was interviewing us.

We used to teach poetry, now it's theory.
There's no longer room in the system
for a mind as romantic as Henry's.

On a day when snow has fallen
lightly, sprinkling the ground,
and a flock of small birds
are hopping and flying about,
a poem returns to haunt me.

"As you have wasted your life here in this place
You have wasted it in every part of the world."

I am disturbed by the words
of a man I never knew, who lived
in a country I have never visited.
How is it he knows about me,
and that I have not lived
for the good of others, putting their needs
before my own? That I have not been
a perfect husband and father.
That I have not written a book
that graces every other coffee table,
or made a discovery or invention
that will save lives and relieve human suffering?

How can he say I have wasted my life?
What can he possibly know about me?
And yet I see that he does.

## SHOO-FLY PIE

The plain-faced Mennonite woman
with her little white cap
selling cheese and shoo-fly pie . . .

Existence can be so peaceful —
you only have to be good.
What am I doing here?

At Lewisburg, where I am,
Route 15 runs by a graveyard.
On the one hand there's the road,
cars, trucks, vans, tractor trailers
going by. On the other,
those who lie still.

I saw the name "Middlesworth"
and "M Potato Chips"
on the side of a van.
Twenty minutes later
the name "Middlesworth" again,
cut in stone: "Mary A." and "Dallas B."

But my dear Muse is yawning.
She's bored with my notes.
She wants me to pay attention
to her. And even then . . .
I hear her voice: "So it's gratitude
you want!" And, "That's not what I said."
And finally, "You don't understand."

It's no use looking at stones
named Yoder, Noll, and Person.
I thought that the name Brocius
might yield something: Isaac A.
and Henrietta B.
He was born in 1843
and served in the Civil War.

To the right of MOTHER
four little tombstones stand
at attention, sounding off:
Annie   Arthur   Henry   John.
A story might be made of this
but what would it mean to me?

✦

Well, what did I expect
in a graveyard? Go to life
and talk to the ruddy farmer
on his tractor plowing a field
for corn and oats. See how he carves
the earth eighteen inches deep
with his blades . . . how daintily
he lifts them when he passes
over the grass he wants to leave
unplowed. The soil he's turned
lies thick and steaming, scallops
of rich, brown Mother Nature.
See him going over it again
with the discs. How he rakes,
and spreads "Gold Special Starter
2-4-2." It's not his fertilizer
that smells, he assures us,
but the sewage plant on the hill.

Here comes one of his sons,
four feet high, to lend a hand,
and his wife with the car, bringing lunch.
This is life, and it's real.
But I'd have to see it in writing,
as verse, to know if it works.

✦

We go to the Farmers' Market,
look at potatoes, tomatoes,
cauliflower, beans, and sauerkraut.
And flowers . . . the Azaleas,
Sky Rockets, and Clematis.
Then we enter the long shed
with its aisles and counters piled
with food: nine kinds of cheese
at least, and nine of pie.
There are Sticky Buns and Donuts. . . .

Look at the meat, all the sausages,
Country Style, Fresh, and Smoked;
Pork Chops, Ham Shanks, Spare Ribs,
Scrapple, Sirloin Roast.
Your mind reels with the variety
of ways of eating animals.
As I look around at the people
pushing by, no one, it seems
weighs less than three hundred pounds.

There go Rump Roast and Porterhouse Steak.
In front of me, an enormous sow
carrying a bunch of flowers . . .
The male equally magnificent
in a red-check shirt . . . Pig Stomach
overflowing his belt. As I pass
I hear them grunting love-words.
So there's no need to feel sorry
for Ground Chuck and Ham Ends
and Mary's Little Lamb:
they died but rise again
as bellies, backsides, and jowls.

The poetry of life . . .
how impossible it seems!
Wouldn't it be nice to be mindless
and just write, like a "language poet."

"Stop!" she says,
"You're beginning to digress."

She's right. I must be tired.
Some other day . . . when I'm not trying,
perhaps, I'll make sense of it all.

"It's good to be back,"
I said to the checkout girl.
"I've been in Hawaii."
"That'll be forty-seven dollars,"
she said, "and twenty-three cents."

"Life," said Joe Butensky,
"is like a glass of tea."
If you asked him why,
"How do I know?" he would say.
"Am I a philosopher?"

I was reminded of Joe
the other day on the subway.
Sitting across from me
was a woman wearing a jacket
with the 82nd Airborne patch,
pants of glistening spandex,
and running shoes. Two wires
hung from her head to the stereo
she was holding in her lap.

I thought of Joe. Don't ask me
why. Am I a philosopher?

# THE POET'S PIPE

I am a poet's pipe,
The modernistic kind,
Not a churchwarden type
But elegantly lined.

Straight stem and simple bowl,
No grinning Gothic skull,
Nor Chinese rigmarole,
Nor buxom Turkish trull.

I read him like a book
(e.g., I know just where
He got this poem. Look
In the pages of Corbière.)

"Cast off!" he shouts. "Full steam!"
Aye, aye. I'm burning red.
Life is a waking dream
Until he goes to bed.

His devils in dark swarms
Fly from my smoking spout.
Bright, intellectual forms
Are hovering about.

And then his light goes out.

# FAME

"What a thing to be in the Mouth
of Fame," Keats says in a letter.
I gaze at the Blue Atlas Cedar
by my window, where Veronica,
our brave little Westie, lies.
*Requiescat in pace.*
She used to wait by the door
in the morning, and lead the way
to my study, and lie there all day.
Ron didn't care about fame,
she liked the sound of the typewriter.

As I gaze out the window
Miriam and Custis Lee
are walking toward the house.
She is holding a bunch of daffodils,
bright yellow against the green.
And if someone were to say,
"In another generation
you'll be gone, and so will they,
leaving not a mark to show
that you ever lived."

So what?

I had come to Australia
for ten weeks, as a guest of the state.
My duties were light: to confer
with students. They didn't want to —
they came once or twice, that was all.

One night someone knocked: a student
with some poems she'd like me to see.
The next day I observed her
in the dining room, and went over.
"I liked" I began to say . . .
She lifted her hands, imploring me
not to speak. All around her
they were talking about the usual subjects,
motorbikes and football.
If it got around that she wrote poems . . .

At night I would sit in my room
reading, keeping a journal,
and, with the aid of a map,
trying to learn the positions
of the southern constellations.
I'd look at them on the map,
then go outside and try to find them
in the sky, before I forgot.

I had recently been divorced
and was starting a new life,
as they say. The world lies before you,

where to live and what to be.
A fireman? An explorer?
An astronaut? Then you look in the mirror.
It was night sweats. Listening
to an echo of the end.

✦

Roger had a live-in girlfriend.
They asked if I'd like to go with them
to a party, and sleep over.

He drove. I looked at the gum trees.
Not the Outback, but country . . .
cattle and kangaroos,
and flies, getting in your eyes,
ears, nose, and mouth.
Once, talking to a sheepherder,
I watched a fly crawl over his face
from his eye to his mouth,
and start walking back
before he brushed it off.
They learn to put up with nature
and not make a fuss like us.

We arrived. I was introduced,
and they made up a bed for me
on the porch at the back.
Then the party began to arrive:

Australians, lean and athletic.
They put a tape on the stereo,
turned it up full blast,
and danced, or stood and shouted
to each other above the noise,

I danced with two or three women
and tried shouting. Then I went
and sat on the bed on the porch.
There was nowhere to go, no door
I could close to shut out the noise.

✦

So I went for a walk
in the dark, away from the sound.
There were gum trees, wind rustling
the leaves. Or was it snakes?

There are several venomous kinds.
The taipan. There's a story
about a child who was sitting
on a log and fell backward
onto a taipan. It struck him
twenty-three times.
There's the tiger snake and the brown.
When they have finished telling you
about snakes, they start on spiders.

You don't need these — you have only to walk
into the bush. There are stories
about campers who did, and were lost
and never seen again.

All this was on my mind.
I stepped carefully, keeping the lights
of the house behind me in sight.
And when I saw a clearing
in the trees, I walked to it.

✦

I stood in the middle of the clearing
looking at the sky. It was glittering
with unknown constellations.
Everything I had ever known
seemed to have disappeared.
And who was I, standing there
in the middle of Australia
at night? I had ceased to exist.
There was only whatever it was
that was looking at the sky
and listening to the wind.

After a while I broke away
and went back to the lights and the party.
A month later I left Australia.

But ever since, to this day,
there has been a place in my mind,
a clearing in the shadows,
and above it, stars and constellations
so bright and thick they seem to rustle.
And beyond them . . . infinite space,
eternity, you name it.

There's nothing that stands between me
and it, whatever it is.